PETERBOROUGH

A STORY OF CITY AND COUNTRY, PEOPLE AND PLACES

THE PETERBOROUGH LANDSCAPE IS FORMED

There has been a brick-making industry in Peterborough for over a hundred years, but few people realise that the foundations of that industry were laid down in the Jurassic Age, 150 million years ago. At that time, most of the British Isles did not exist, and many of the rocks we now see were being slowly deposited as sediments at the bottom of sub-tropical seas. One of those rock formations was the Oxford clay, formed from mud washed in from surrounding land, which came to be used in the brick industry.

The seas swarmed with strange animals, including the coiled ammonites so familiar to fossil-hunters today, huge marine reptiles like plesiosaurs, ichthyosaurs and crocodiles, and fish. Sometimes when these creatures died, their skeletons were preserved in the mud at the bottom of the sea, to be buried deeper by later sediments.

This process continued for 100 million years until enormous earth movements squeezed up the ocean floor above the surface of the sea. In southern Europe the Alps were formed, and in Britain the ripples of those earth movements pushed the Oxford clay to the surface.

Below: Plesiosaurs are the most abundant of the marine reptiles found in the Oxford clay. Three species are known – all of them have a long neck and small skull.

Upon this Rock ...

The limestones that outcrop to the west of Peterborough are the oldest Jurassic rocks in the area. Many of the older buildings in the city, including the Museum, are made from Ketton or Clipsham stone. The cathedral is built of Barnack ragstone, and some of the effigies are of Alwalton marble, both very shelly limestones. Collyweston slate, also a limestone, can be seen on many roofs. There are numerous abandoned quarries, and some that still extract limestone for buildings, for roadstone and, at Ketton, for cement manufacture.

Right: In 1996 the bones of a straight-tusked elephant were found in the Welland Bank gravel pit. The remains of rhinoceros and hippopotamus have also been found, indicating that around 120,000 years ago the climate in the Peterborough area was very much warmer than today.

Above: *This plesiosaur skeleton is one of the most complete specimens in the world. It was found in the Dogsthorpe brick pit in 1987 and is now on permanent display in Peterborough Museum & Art Gallery.*

Over the next 50 million years the forces of erosion laid bare the ancient rocks that are now to be seen in the brick pits and limestone quarries to the west of the city. Then, in the last few hundred thousand years, a succession of ice sheets scraped off the surface of the land. During the intervening warm periods, when the ice sheets melted, huge quantities of sand and gravel were washed out and left behind in the river valleys and fens.

These gravel deposits are quarried today for building materials, bringing evidence of a landscape that is difficult to imagine. Elephants, rhinoceros, bison, hippopotamus, reindeer and wild oxen roamed, some in the ice tundra, others in the warm inter-glacial periods, and their bones are often found in the gravel pits, together with fragments of plants, fish, beetles, snails and other small forms of life.

Peterborough Museum & Art Gallery houses the skeleton of the 117,000 year old Deeping elephant, several skulls of woolly rhinoceros and the skeleton of the Whittlesey ox. The Geology Gallery has the best display of Jurassic marine reptiles in Britain, outside of London.

Right: *Ammonites abound in the Oxford clay in Peterborough's brick pits. They are usually crushed flat, and are only rarely found as perfectly formed as this one.*

Peterborough's First People

The earliest human remains found in England date back some half a million years. It is not known exactly when human feet first roamed the Peterborough area, but the evidence of flint tools made and discarded do indicate that people were here a few hundred thousand years ago. Many stone hand axes have been found locally, along with the 'waste' flakes produced when chipping tools into shape.

The creators of the earliest of these flint tools were people such as Neanderthals, who were stockier in build than 'modern' humans, and had heavy, prominent faces. 'Modern' humans, people much more like us, became dominant about 35,000 years ago. We know that these people, of the palaeolithic period ('Old Stone Age', *c.*500,000 to *c.*8500 BC), were few in number, and that they were very skilled hunter-gatherers, able to live off the land without any formal method of agriculture.

Left: *A palaeolithic stone hand axe. A fine collection of these very ancient artefacts was recovered from quarries by local antiquary and solicitor G. Wyman Abbott during the early years of the last century.*

The Peterborough area was on the fringe of the glaciers during the last Ice Age, and when it ended, around 10,000 years ago, people moved once more into the thawing landscape. This was probably a very mobile population, following game migrations and seasonal foodstuffs across the country. The river valleys served as hunting grounds and as corridors to ease travel through the heavily wooded landscape.

Rising sea levels, and the sluggish progress of the rivers flowing to the North Sea, caused reed swamp to develop in the Fens. Trees toppled, and were submerged for thousands of years, re-appearing as 'bog oaks' when the Fens were eventually drained.

Farmers and Potters …

Right and Below left: *A neolithic bowl of the 'Mortlake' Peterborough type and (below) an early Bronze Age beaker. Finds like these from gravel workings in the Fengate area, during the early years of the last century, brought Peterborough's prehistoric archaeology to national attention.*

Above: *Palaeolithic hunters stalk their prey in the flood-plain of the River Welland.*

People who occupied this increasingly damp fenland landscape during the earliest part of the neolithic period ('New Stone Age', 4500 to 2000 BC) shared a hunting, fishing and gathering lifestyle similar to that of the preceeding mesolithic period, or Middle Stone Age.

Throughout the neolithic period, however, great changes were to take place. With it came the first evidence of farming – cultivating crops and rearing herds of animals – and of pottery-making. Peterborough and the Fengate area lend their name to distinctive types of neolithic pottery, which are found widely across England.

Excavations in the Fengate area during the 1970s revealed that in the second millennium BC the fen edge was divided up by a network of ditches and hedged banks into droves and small fields or enclosures, among which stood the occasional isolated round building. The enclosure and drove system, which led down from dry ground to the ever wetter fen, was maintained throughout the Bronze Age (2000 to 800 BC), and was probably designed to manage animal herds – specifically flocks of sheep – grazing on the lush fen margins.

The growth of permanently settled communities and their herds in the area put pressure on the natural resources. Large areas of ancient woodland were gradually cleared for pasture and cultivation. As long ago as the neolithic period, trees in the Welland valley were systematically coppiced.

Left: *A temporary camp of early neolithic hunter-gatherers. Scatters of stone tools and tool-making debris are found today in the Fens and along the river valleys.*

Right: *Neolithic and Bronze Age stone tools – a polished axe, sickle blade and arrow head. Tools were often made from local flint, but some were imported from places such as the Lake District.*

5

... Monuments and Mysteries

During the neolithic period, the first monuments began to appear in the landscape. Stonehenge in Wiltshire is world-famous, but few people know that similar monuments were built in the Peterborough area. They were usually circular areas enclosed by ditches and earth banks, and used settings of timber posts rather than large stones. Henges have been discovered at Maxey, and very recently at Whittlesey. Cursus monuments, long rectangular enclosures formed by two parallel banks and ditches, which may extend many kilometres across the landscape, have been revealed at Maxey and at Barnack.

The area also has an exceptionally high concentration of 'causewayed enclosures' or 'causewayed camps', large oval enclosures defined by segments of ditches and banks. The methodical archaeological excavation of one causewayed enclosure between Etton and Maxey produced fascinating insights into neolithic life and religion in the area. Deposits of

Right: *A socketed axe and flanged axe of the Bronze Age. Bronze tools were much more efficient for woodworking than the stone tools of the neolithic, but some also held a symbolic value.*

Above right and Below: *Part of the prehistoric Fengate field system has been reconstructed at Flag Fen. Visitors can walk along droves, through hedged fields and into the thatched huts, which would have been familiar to Bronze Age families in the area.*

Right: *Excavations and air photographs have shown that the Maxey area was part of an amazing neolithic and Bronze Age 'monumental landscape'. The remains of a neolithic cursus, causewayed enclosure, henge and early Bronze Age burial mounds are shown in this interpretation.*

Below: *An early Bronze Age 'Beaker' burial from Barnack. The burial, accompanied by rich grave goods including an archer's wrist guard, was heralded as one of the most important discoveries of its kind and was placed on display in the British Museum.*

stone tools, pottery, animal remains, quern-stones, and even human bones had been placed in the ground as offerings.

The Bronze Age timber alignment and platform at Flag Fen may also have served a ritual purpose. Watery places were often ascribed mystical properties by later prehistoric peoples; valuable items such as weaponry and jewellery were offered to the gods through these conduits to the spiritual world. The significance and use of many of the early monuments is not fully understood, but they do show that prehistoric communities in the area became increasingly settled, and that for thousands of years parts of the landscape were reserved for spiritual purposes.

Above: *The 'island' of Thorney in the Bronze Age, viewed from the east. Tidally influenced creeks meander across the fen floor and peter out in swamps at the edge of the higher land. The tree-like pattern of the creeks can still be traced on aerial photographs.*

Right: *Excavations of the Bronze Age timber alignment on the fen edge at Fengate revealed a great quantity of items. Weapons, some deliberately bent and broken, had been placed in the water alongside the timbers.*

7

Prehistory Gives Way to the Romans

The Iron Age (800 BC to AD 43) saw the introduction of working with iron, a stronger and more durable material than the copper alloys used in the preceding Bronze Age.

During the later Bronze Age and Iron Age, the Fens east of Peterborough continued to grow wetter. Reed swamps gradually enveloped the old burial mounds perched on the fen edge and small fen islands, and eventually the Flag Fen timber platform was submerged. The layers of peat, clay and silt laid down in wet conditions protected these remains, hiding them from view until modern times.

Iron Age people worked the landscape more intensively than their predecessors; their ploughs could cope with heavier soils and their settlements were larger and more numerous. Around Peterborough were clusters of timber-built, thatched, round dwellings surrounded by small fields or paddocks. Such 'open' settlements used mixed farming methods, relying heavily on livestock such as cows and sheep. However, discarded animal bones found at an Iron Age settlement site in the Fengate area in the 1970s showed that wild animals such as deer and otter, and wildfowl including swan, pelican, crane and stork, were caught in the surrounding Fens.

Above: *The offering of precious items into watery places continued into the Iron Age. Iron swords and other items have been discovered in an old channel of the River Nene at Orton Longueville.*

Borough Fen

Some Iron Age settlements were enclosed by protective earthworks. A small rectangular enclosure containing at least two buildings, protected by a deep ditch, was excavated at Werrington in 1979. A large near-circular earthwork with two ditch circuits and banks survives at Borough Fen. It was built on the edge of the fen and is among the best-preserved Iron Age sites in the country.

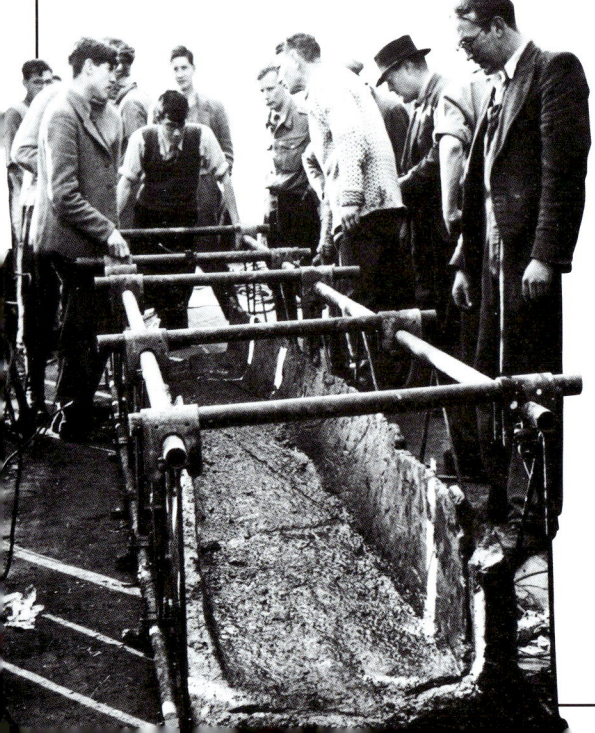

Left: *An Iron Age dugout canoe was found in mud below the River Nene near the Town Bridge in 1950. Prehistoric boats have also been found near Whittlesey; they were an effective way of moving through the watery landscape.*

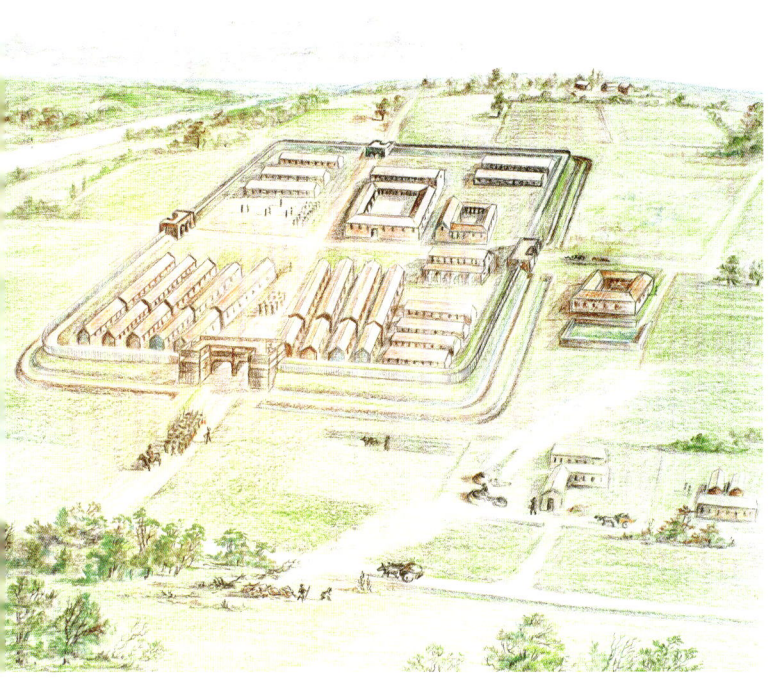

Above: *Roman builders used clay tiles for roofs, drains and heating systems. This tile, found near Barnack, is stamped with the name of the Ninth Legion, whose garrisons would have required great quantities of building materials.*

Left: *An interpretation of the Longthorpe Roman fortress. The fortress was occupied soon after the Roman invasion, and was probably modified during the Boudiccan Revolt. It now lies beneath a golf course.*

Late Iron Age Britain was divided into distinct tribal areas or kingdoms. Peterborough lay between the Catuvellauni to the south and the Corieltauvi to the north, with the Iceni to the east. After their arrival on the south coast in AD 43, the Roman army pushed north.

Southern tribes such as the Catuvellauni and Iceni generally adapted more readily to Roman rule than those of the north. In AD 60, however, when Rome attempted to exert greater control over their 'client kingdom', the Iceni revolted. Led by Boudicca, the Iceni and other tribes 'had no thought of taking prisoners or selling them as slaves … but only of slaughter, the gibbet, fire and cross.'

The main north–south route of eastern Roman Britain, Ermine Street, ran through the Peterborough area. Another major Roman route, the Fen Causeway – actually a system of roads, causeways and canals – ran across the fens from Norfolk. A fort was built to guard Ermine Street's crossing of the Nene at Water Newton, and a larger fort was constructed at Longthorpe. It is possible that it was from the Longthorpe fort that the ill-fated Ninth Legion set out to relieve Boudicca's siege of Colchester. Tacitus, the Roman historian, describes their infamous defeat and the survivors' hasty retreat to the safety of their fortification.

THE ROMANS MAKE THEIR MARK

Buried Treasure

This collection of late Roman silver forms part of a magnificent hoard discovered at Durobrivae in 1974. The items bear Christian symbols and almost certainly comprise the oldest church plate known anywhere in the Roman world. The hoard was buried around the middle of the 4th century AD – it is interesting to speculate why it was hidden, and why its owners were never able to recover this great treasure.

In more peaceful times, settlement flourished. A town, Durobrivae (meaning 'fortress bridge') grew up on the banks of the Nene – not on the site of the present city of Peterborough, but a few miles upstream. The earthwork remains of the walled part of the town may be traced in a large pasture just off the A1. Durobrivae probably became a regional capital and market centre. There were significant smaller towns at Casterton near Stamford, Ashton near Oundle, and large villages and an administrative centre near March.

Rich villas and farmsteads were built in the productive countryside around Peterborough.

Many of these sites were occupied in the Iron Age, but were rebuilt according to Roman fashion as the native population adopted a Roman lifestyle. In later Roman times, the Nene valley became the centre of a major pottery industry. The distinctive white clay pots, which were given a grey or reddish-brown 'slip' (or colour-coat), were traded widely across Britain. They are now known as 'Castor Ware' or 'Nene Valley Ware'. Iron ore was extracted from the limestone deposits surrounding the Nene valley and worked in hearths fuelled by charcoal from local woodland.

The Fens, too, were very well developed in the Roman period, perhaps under direct imperial control. Extensive settlements and field systems were constructed on low islands, and many perched on the exposed banks (or 'roddons') of the old prehistoric rivers. Salt was extracted from tidal rivers which sometimes still ran far inland. The Car Dyke, a massive ditch or canal of which

Below: *E.T. Artis, house steward to the Fitzwilliams at Milton Hall and celebrated Peterborough antiquarian, recorded his discoveries in a book of beautiful illustrations, published in 1828. This plate shows the excavation of Roman building remains at Castor.*

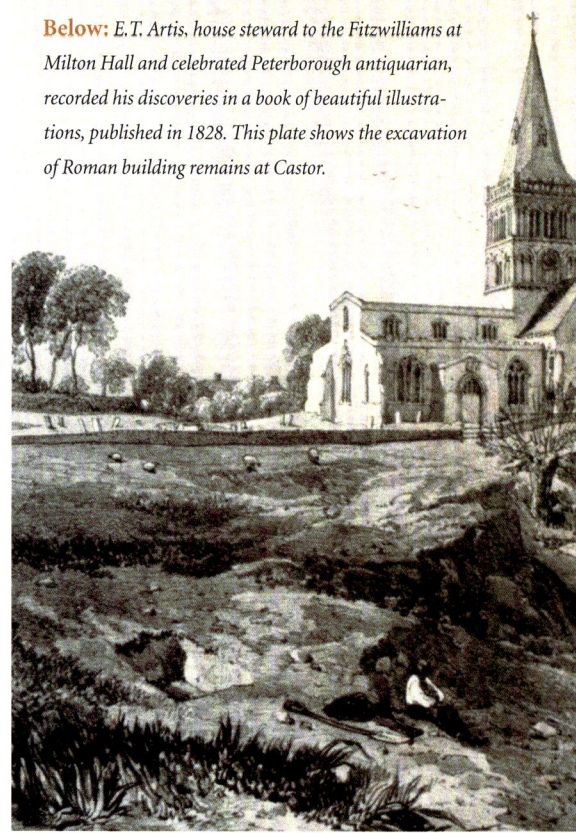

Left: *The potteries around Peterborough produced distinctive high-quality Roman tablewares that were sold throughout the country. 'Hunt cups' are named after the chase scenes depicted on them – here the hare is running from two hounds.*

Above: *The excavation of Roman houses and cemeteries in the area has produced interesting insights into everyday life. Some finds, like this comb, indicate the importance of personal grooming and appearance in Roman Britain!*

Below left: *Fragments of painted wall-plaster from colourful frescoes are found at many Roman sites in the area, and some spectacular mosaic floors have been revealed. This mosaic, excavated by E.T. Artis in 1827, adorned a villa near Helpston.*

Above: *The town of Durobrivae during the 4th century AD. Much of the town was enclosed by defences, but large areas of settlement and industry thrived outside. A palace overlooked the Nene from the hillside on which Castor now sits.*

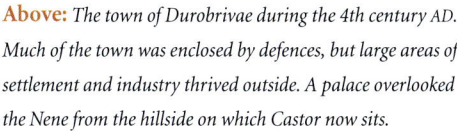

substantial lengths still survive, was constructed along the fen edge east of Peterborough.

Something of the importance of the Peterborough area to Roman Britain is reflected in the density and richness of the archaeological remains found here. At Castor during the 1820s, Edmund Tyrell Artis investigated a series of substantial Roman buildings adorned with mosaics and featuring all the trappings of wealthy Roman society. Fragments of massive Roman walls may still be seen in Stocks Hill and Church Hill at Castor. This extraordinary complex has been interpreted as the palace of a Roman dignitary, as yet unidentified – perhaps an official involved with the administration of the pottery industry, the town of Durobrivae, or the imperial estate in the Fens?

11

Settlers and Saints

The Anglo-Saxon way of life in the Peterborough area was very different to that of the Romano-British. The great pottery industries that flourished along the Nene valley in the 4th century AD were abandoned in the 5th century. The town of Durobrivae was not maintained, and gradually was forgotten. The grand Roman buildings at Castor, and countless villas in the surrounding countryside, were left to fall down, or were robbed for their stone. The shells or sites of some of these Roman buildings, however, were re-occupied by Anglo-Saxon families or continued to be occupied by the native families, albeit eventually in the Anglo-Saxon fashion.

Above: *Discovered by metal detector near Castor, this 'hanging bowl' was the possession of an Anglo-Saxon noble. It is made of bronze, and decorated with enamel inlaid discs and animal-headed hanging brackets.*

Left: *This painting, commissioned for the BBC television series* Meet the Ancestors, *is based on an individual from the early Anglo-Saxon cemetery at Alwalton.*

Below: *Pre-Christian Anglo-Saxons in the Peterborough area took treasured possessions with them to the grave. Spears, knives and shields are found in men's graves, and women's graves often contain jewellery, like this bronze cruciform brooch.*

Early and Middle Anglo-Saxon settlements generally comprised small clusters of timber houses, rather than substantial villages. Such settlements have been excavated at Woodston, Orton Longueville and Maxey. Evidence of Anglo-Saxon craftsmanship can be seen in the spectacular artefacts found in cemeteries, such as those excavated at Woodston, Gunthorpe and Alwalton.

The Peterborough area lay on the boundary of two great Anglo-Saxon kingdoms, Mercia, to the west, and East Anglia. The abbey at Peterborough was founded by Mercian royalty during the second half of the 7th century and came to acquire large amounts of land. With the abbey came also the beginnings of the settlement that would eventually grow to become the medieval town.

What's in a Name?

The years before the Norman Conquest saw the origins of villages still recognisable today. They have descriptive Anglo-Saxon or Anglo-Scandinavian names: Eye ('Island or high land in the marsh'); Upton ('higher farmstead/village'); Orton ('farmstead by a ridge or bank'); Thornhaugh ('thorn tree enclosure'); Fletton ('farmstead on a stream'); Maxey ('island of a man named Maccus'); Sutton ('south farmstead' – Anglo-Saxon); and Southorpe ('south outlying farmstead' – Anglo-Scandinavian).

Above: *Barnack church tower is a rare surviving example of late Anglo-Saxon architecture. There were important limestone quarries at Barnack during late Saxon and medieval times; the durable stone was used to build many churches throughout the region.*

The settlement at Peterborough was originally named Medeshamstede. It was renamed 'Burh' in the late 10th century after it was enclosed by a wall and ditch. 'Burh' was an Anglo-Saxon term applied to fortified places. Later on it became known as 'Burh St Peter', from which was derived the present-day name 'Peterborough'.

William the Conqueror's armies were frustrated by rebellion in the fens long after much of England had been subdued. Hereward the Wake, who became the most famous of the English resistance leaders, fought a guerrilla war against the Normans in the fens. Anticipating the arrival of Peterborough's new Norman abbot and his soldiers, a Danish fleet, with Hereward's support, attacked the burh and looted the abbey's treasures.

Fair or Foul?

Early in the 8th century St Guthlac came to dwell as a hermit on the island at Crowland. His biographer painted the fens as a wild, hostile, demon-haunted wilderness, '… a most dismal fen of immense size. It is a very long tract, now consisting of marshes, now of bogs, sometimes of black waters overhung by fog, sometimes studded with wooded islands and traversed by the windings of tortuous streams.'

On the other hand, Hugh Candidus, Peterborough's medieval chronicler, described the fenland as 'very valuable to men because there are obtained in abundance all things needful for them that dwell thereby, logs and stubble for kindling, hay for the feeding of their beasts, thatch for roofing of their houses, and many other things of use and profit, and moreover it is very full of fish and fowl'. He concluded that 'this Burh is built in a fair spot, and a goodly, because on the one side it is rich in fenland, and in goodly waters, and on the other it has abundance of ploughlands and woodlands, with many fertile meads and pastures. On all sides it is beautiful to look upon …'.

Above: *The unique 'Monks Stone' or 'Hedda Stone', housed in the cathedral, is a fine example of Anglo-Saxon craftsmanship. Important sculptures of similar date (around AD 800) survive at Castor and Fletton.*

A Medieval New Town

Hugh Candidus summed up Peterborough's fortunes after the Conquest by lamenting 'that city which was called the Golden Borough became the poorest of cities.' Following the violent events of 1069, the king gave the abbey the exceptionally onerous responsibility of supporting sixty knights. While theoretically this made the Abbot of Peterborough one of the mightiest Churchmen in the country, it was a considerable strain on the abbey's estates. In the mid 12th century, however, the resourceful Abbot Martin de Bec planned a new settlement to the west of the abbey gates. Earlier settlement had been cramped within the walls of the burh, and outside its walls to the north-east in the Boongate area. The present Cathedral Square (the former Market Place), Long Causeway and Bridge Street, which ran down to wharves (or hithes) on the River Nene, were all elements of the medieval new town. At this time

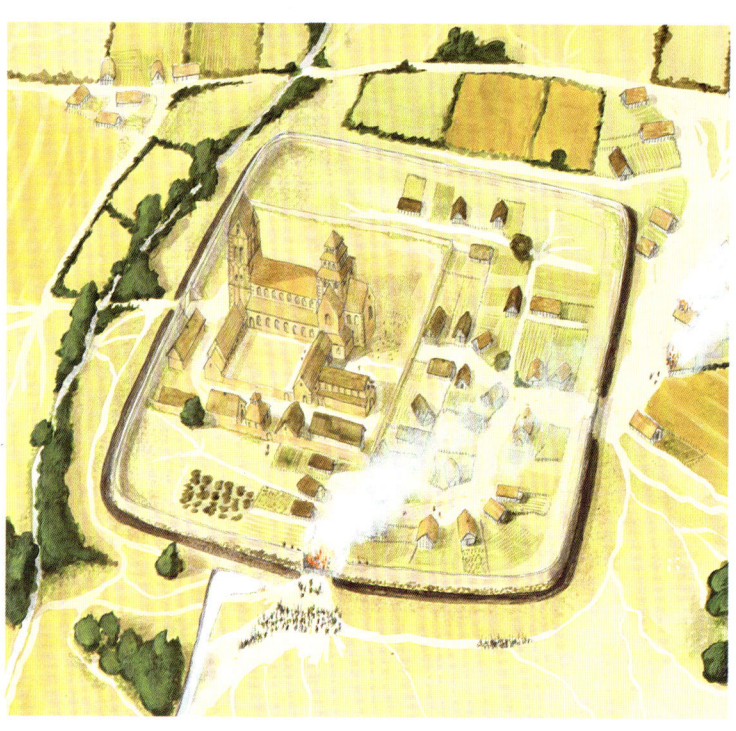

Above: *A view of the burh and abbey at Peterborough during the attack by Hereward and the Danes in 1070. Fighting took place at the Bolhithe Gate and resulted in the destruction of the town.*

the monastic church – the present cathedral – was also re-planned on a much larger scale. A great deal of the 12th-century building remains; indeed, the interior of Peterborough Cathedral is one of the best places in Britain to appreciate the splendid architecture of this period. The famous painted ceiling of the nave dates to around 1230.

Further changes to take place in Peterborough during the later Middle Ages included the construction of the Town Bridge in 1307. This timber bridge, which stood immediately up-stream of the present Town Bridge, was ruined during the following winter but quickly rebuilt. During the early 15th century, a new parish church, dedicated to St John the Baptist, was built at the west end of the Market Place, replacing one that had served the old settlement around Boongate. It is said that excavation and removal of the tainted ground around the medieval butchers' stalls in the Market Place created the hole in which the church now stands.

Above: *The great tower of the impressive medieval residence at Longthorpe was built about 1300. Its interior is adorned with the finest surviving set of medieval domestic wall paintings in the country.*

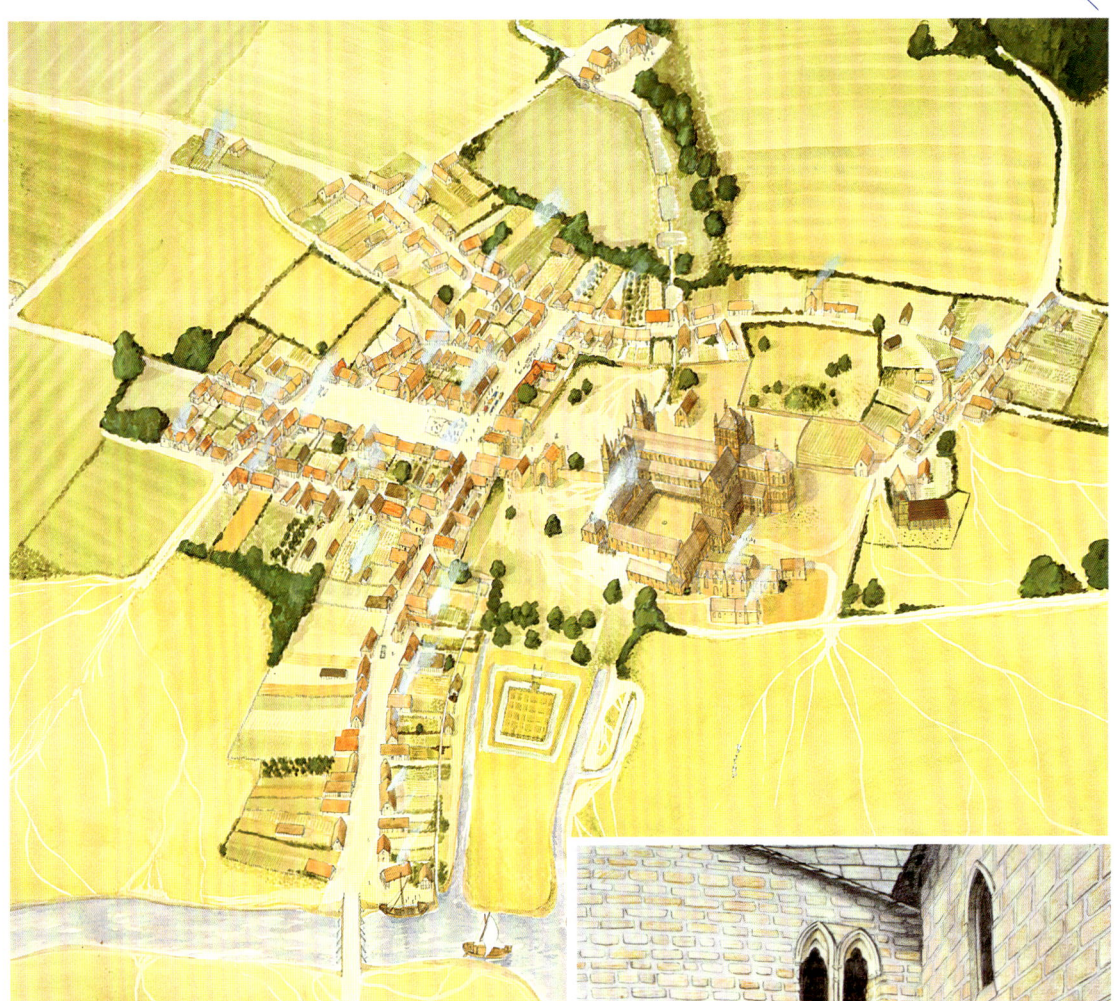

Above: *An impression of Peterborough during the 14th century. Peterborough's modern centre disguises much of its ancient past, but parts of the medieval town are still recognisable in today's street plan.*

The outlying villages were surrounded by the medieval 'open' field systems, common throughout England. The distinctive traces of medieval 'ridge and furrow' agriculture have all but disappeared across the area, but survive in small pockets here and there. The land was managed from the abbey's granges (or principal farms), such as those at Eyebury, Oxney, Northolm, Singlesole and Tanholt, near Eye, and from manors. Fortified manors were built at Maxey, Helpston, Northborough and at Woodcroft Castle (also near Helpston). Substantial parts of the latter two remain, and the sites of the former may be traced in earthwork remains.

Above: *This medieval yard off Narrow Bridge Street survived until the 20th century. The 13th-century window above the street entrance is preserved at Peterborough Museum & Art Gallery.*

From Abbey to Cathedral, from Town to City

Tudor Peterborough was a flourishing town, still dominated by the abbey; but in the 1530s, Henry VIII's Church reforms were to bring enormous changes.

Katharine of Aragon, Henry's first wife, eventually moved to Kimbolton Castle, south of Peterborough, after her divorce. She died there in 1536, and was buried at Peterborough. Henry's dissolution of the monasteries in 1539 included Peterborough Abbey, but it was saved from destruction and designated a cathedral. It is said that Henry

Above: *Katharine of Aragon was buried in the abbey on 29 January 1536. Peterborough is now twinned with Alcala de Henares, where Katharine was born, and a remembrance service is held every January in the cathedral.*

Above: *In 1508, the last major addition to the abbey church was completed. Still known today as the 'New Building', this chapel has a beautiful fan-vaulted ceiling, probably designed by John Wastell, architect of the famous King's College Chapel in Cambridge.*

Mary Queen of Scots

In 1585 the Catholic Mary Queen of Scots was imprisoned by her Protestant cousin, Elizabeth I, at Fotheringay Castle, 8 miles from Peterborough. On Elizabeth's orders, Mary was executed there in February 1587. She was buried in Peterborough Cathedral, but her body was removed to Westminster Abbey in 1612 by her son, James I.

Robert Scarlett

A celebrated figure in Tudor Peterborough was Robert Scarlett, the cathedral sexton (gravedigger), who lived to be 98. He buried both Katharine of Aragon and Mary Queen of Scots, and also claimed to have buried two members of each Peterborough household during his life. It has even been suggested that Shakespeare based his graveyard scene in Hamlet around this colourful character.

looked favourably upon Peterborough because it was Katharine's resting place, but greater influences were probably the co-operation shown by the last abbot (who became the first bishop), and Peterborough's location. The town became a city, with the right to elect two members of Parliament. Although the power of the Church now began to wane, the Bishop, Dean and Chapter kept law and order in city and country through regular 'courts'.

Also involved in local affairs were the church wardens, and religious guilds who gave alms to the poor. In 1547 these were confiscated by Henry VIII and their lands sold off, but in Peterborough three citizens – Thomas Robinson, Jeremy Green and Robert Mallory – bought up the lands and carried on the charitable work. When Mallory died in 1572, the guild property was passed to 14 local men who continued to run the charities, becoming known as the Feoffees.

The old monastic abbey school was refounded by Henry VIII in 1541 and renamed 'King's School'. It provided an education for 'twenty poor boys, both destitute of the help of friends and endowed with minds apt for learning …'.

Most local people worked on the land, or were tradesmen. Records suggest that Gilbert Bull, the town baker, may have been a rebellious character – he was fined in 1575 for refusing to allow his loaves of bread to be weighed, and again in 1580 for allowing his pigs to wander the streets.

The power of the wealthier local families, who had bought up church lands, grew in the reign of Elizabeth I. Burghley House was built by William Cecil (later Lord Burghley), the Queen's Secretary of State and closest adviser. In 1576 Elizabeth passed the title of Lord Paramount of the Liberty of Peterborough from the Bishop of Peterborough to Lord Burghley, whose descendants still hold this title today.

Below: *Burghley House was built between 1555 and 1587. Sir William Cecil's descendants still live in the house, which is now open to the public. The grounds are the venue for the famous Burghley Horse Trials.*

Civil War and a Return to Peace

The 1600s were a time of change and upheaval for the people of Peterborough. When Civil War broke out, Peterborough's community was divided as the citizens declared their loyalty to either the Royalists or the Parliamentarians. The city lay on the border of the Eastern Association of counties, which sided with Parliament, and the war reached Peterborough in 1643 when Parliamentary soldiers arrived in the city to attack Royalist strongholds at Stamford and Crowland. The Royalist forces were defeated within a few weeks, and they retired to Burghley House, where they were captured and sent to Cambridge. While the Parliamentary soldiers

Below: *The Guildhall was built on the site of the old Market Cross in the Market Place.*

Right: *This turtle shell is decorated with the arms of Sir Humphrey Orme. It is said that Sir Humphrey, an important local businessman and city MP, supplied the turtle for soup eaten to celebrate the completion of the Guildhall in 1672.*

Above: *The north side of Peterborough Cathedral in 1712. In 1698 Celia Fiennes recorded 'the Cathedrall is a magnificent building', but earlier damage must still have been visible, as Browne Willis wrote in 1718 'scarce any Cathedral in England is more neglected'.*

were in Peterborough, however, they ransacked the cathedral, destroying the high altar and choir stalls, as well as medieval decoration and documents.

Parliament disposed of Church property to raise money for the army and navy. Oliver St John, a Lord Chief Justice who supported Parliament, bought the lease of the Manor of Longthorpe and built Thorpe Hall. In 1654 author John Evelyn described it as 'a stately place … built out of the ruins of the Bishop's Palace and Cloisters'.

The restoration of King Charles II in 1660 led to a new stability and prosperity across the country, and in 1669 the people of Peterborough decided to raise a public subscription 'for the building of a public cross or Town House'. This building, now known as the Guildhall, was erected on the site of the old Market Cross, or 'Butter Cross'.

Throughout history, people sought to work both with and against nature to get the most out of the challenging fenland environment. Morton's Leam, which still survives and now forms the southern boundary of the Nene Wash, was the most ambitious of a long list of medieval drainage and flood protection schemes.

Alms for the Poor

The welfare of the poor at this time was left to the Feoffees, using income from the Town Lands, as their records from 1633 show:

To Emma Biggs a very poore woman whose husband is gone from her and hath left 2 children to be kept by the town and are almost starved … **12d.**

Given to Seaton a very poor man whose legges are swelled with working in the wet fen … **12d.**

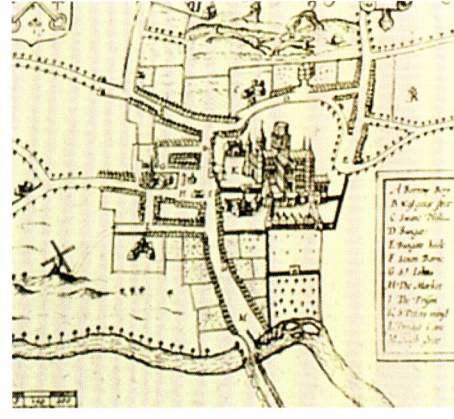

Above: *The earliest map of the city of Peterborough, drawn by John Speed and published in 1610 as part of his map of Northamptonshire.*

It was dug in the later years of the 15th century to take the Nene water directly out to the sea at Wisbech. It was not until the 17th century, however, that schemes for the drainage of the whole 'Great Level' of the fens were begun. In an agreement of 1630, Francis Earl of Bedford, who owned a large fenland estate at Thorney, joined with other 'adventurers' (so-called because they had invested or 'adventured' money in the schemes) and Sir Cornelius Vermuvden, the experienced Dutch engineer, to undertake the work and divide up the proceeds. Originally, the work was to take only six years; in fact, this was just the beginning of an amazing engineering adventure which continues to this day.

Below: *Thorpe Hall, one of the finest surviving Commonwealth mansions in Britain, is now run by the Sue Ryder Foundation as a hospice. The gardens, which retain much of their original layout, are open to the public.*

Above: *This beadwork box is decorated with designs from pattern books of the 1600s. Beadwork was a popular hobby for wealthy women at this time.*

Prosperity and Puddles

During the long Georgian age (1714–1830), Peterborough continued to develop as a busy market centre, benefiting from the rich agricultural land that surrounded the city. The fens were by now being drained, but Daniel Defoe wrote in 1724 that wagons laden with wild duck were still being sent to London twice a week.

Above: *The Squires were a prosperous Peterborough family during the late 18th century. Nathan Fielding has portrayed the young Wright Thomas Squire and his sister Charlotte on a pony in front of their house near the Town Bridge.*

The city's excellent transport links did much to encourage its prosperity, although the roads themselves were often rough and dangerous. Between 1750 and 1840 many local roads were improved by Turnpike Trusts, which collected money from road users at toll gates. Within the city, however, the streets were dirty and difficult to negotiate, and wealthy visitors hired sedan chairs to carry them – indeed, the use of sedan chairs continued in Peterborough long after they went out of fashion elsewhere. It was not until 1790 that the Peterborough Pavement and Improvement Commission was set up specifically to improve the city's streets.

The River Nene had long played an important part in the life of the city. From 1761, after improvements upstream, the river was properly navigable from the seaport of Wisbech as far as Northampton. Much of Northamptonshire's agricultural output was carried down-river, while up-river came produce from north-east England and from Northern Europe – coal and building materials, especially timber, slate and glass.

The Militia lists of 1762 show that most local people still worked on the land, most commonly as labourer, farmer or shepherd. Local trades also prospered, and carpenter, shoemaker, butcher, blacksmith, baker, mason and boatman were all popular occupations. The very poor continued to receive money from the Feoffees, or to be housed in the workhouse. In 1744 Edward Wortley Montague, a city

Horse Racing and High Jinks

The Georgian era was renowned as a time of gracious living for the wealthy. The highlight of the social season in Peterborough was the horse racing which took place in June on the Common (now Fengate), attracting aristocratic visitors. Other entertainments were staged for the people flocking to the city – plays were performed, and there was cock-fighting at the Angel Inn.

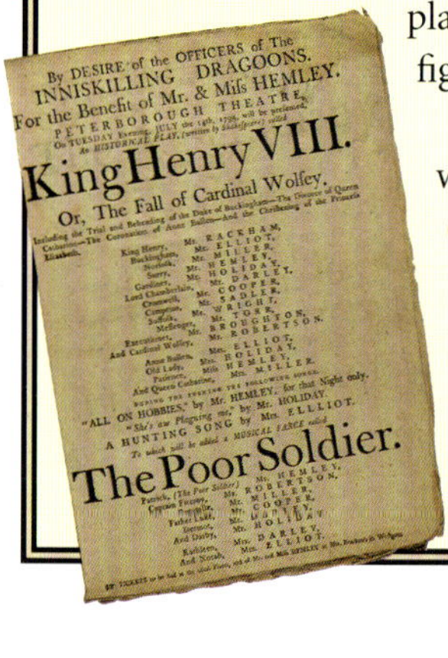

For the less well-off, the Bridge Fair was held over three days in September (October since 1878), while another popular amusement was bull-running in the Market Place. This pastime, and the gambling and drinking that accompanied it, were recorded in 1792 as nuisances in need of controlling.

20

Above: Nathan Fielding's portrayal of the Market Place in 1795. A regular market was held on this site for over 800 years until the stalls were moved to an indoor market nearby in 1963.

MP, built a new workhouse in Westgate 'for the better accommodation of the poor of St John's parish'.

Law and order were controlled by the cathedral's Dean and Chapter through their Court of Petty Sessions, and by the Lord Paramount of the Liberty of Peterborough (the Marquis of Exeter at Burghley House) through the Soke Court. The Lord Paramount maintained a prison in part of the old Abbey buildings. Most prisoners were held inside a wooden cage divided into two cells, but those accused of serious crimes were put in the 'condemned' cell.

Punishments were still harsh at this time, and the last public flogging was recorded in 1819 when a man accused of stealing was flogged by the constable in the Marketstede. In 1820 the gallows were moved to Fengate from their old site on the road to Millfield.

Prisoners and Treasures

In 1797 a prison was built at Norman Cross, near Peterborough, to hold prisoners, mostly French, of the Napoleonic Wars (1793–1815). At times, as many as 7,000 prisoners were held in what was perhaps the world's first custom-built Prisoner of War camp. Many local traders and farmers supplied food and other goods to the prison, while the prisoners themselves earned an income from the sale of caskets and models made from bone and straw. The bone mechanical model (above) is part of a collection of such items in the Peterborough Museum & Art Gallery.

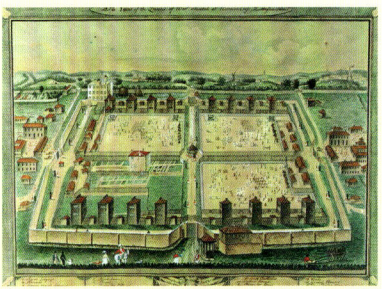

Above: A watercolour painting of the prison camp or 'depot' at Norman Cross. The prison was divided into quadrants, which each contained the prisoners' quarters and a large exercise yard. Barracks for the guards were built outside the prison's east and west gates.

21

A Tribute to a Rural Tradition

Above: *An engraving of John Clare in 1820, aged 27, when his first book was published.*

Above: *Haymaking at Paston near Peterborough in the 1890s. For some time, traditional farming methods continued alongside new developments.*

The late 18th and 19th centuries saw great changes to the old rural way of life, for this was the age of the Industrial Revolution. Many people left the countryside to look for work in the cities. Ancient common fields were divided up and enclosed by hedges, and the character of the countryside changed forever.

Into this dynamic period was born John Clare, the son of a farm labourer, at Helpston near Peterborough, in 1793. In the 1820s, Clare's first book of poetry, *Poems Descriptive of Rural Life and Scenery,* was published, celebrating the rural tradition and everyday life of country people and animals. He is perhaps best known today for his collection *The Shepherd's Calendar.* In his words for January, he shuts out the harsh winter and enjoys the family hearth:

Above: *A fenland spade, used to make and maintain the dykes that drained the fens. Fenland farming involved a constant struggle to control the water levels.*

> The shutter closd the lamp alight
> The faggot chopt and blazing bright
> The shepherd from his labour free
> Dancing his children on his knee

John Clare developed a mental illness and spent the last 22 years of his life in Northampton Asylum; but his love of the country lived on in his poetry, and he remains a famous English poet.

The Railway Age

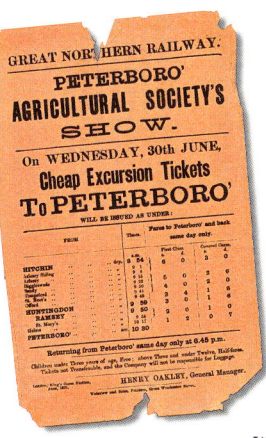

The railway arrived in Peterborough in 1845 with what later became known as the East Station, to link Peterborough with the London and Birmingham Railway. Other lines followed over the next five years and in 1850 the North Station opened, on the site of the present main line station, when the Great Northern Railway line reached the city of London. From the 1850s to the 1960s Peterborough was a nationally important railway centre with a locomotive depot and engineering works plus some 80 miles of sidings, creating many new jobs and bringing huge growth and prosperity to an already thriving city. By 1901 the railway industry employed 25% of the city's adult male population.

Over 260 new houses were built just north of the city between 1854 and 1866 for the railway workers, in an area that came to be called 'New England'. It is still known by this name today.

Above: *This painting, based on a Victorian photograph, shows the city centre. The office of the Great Northern Railway Receiving Service can be seen to the left of the Great Gate. Parcels sent by rail were collected from here.*

The railway encouraged many people to travel further afield – in 1851 day trippers could leave Peterborough at 7 a.m. on the Great Northern Railway to visit the Great Exhibition in London, paying 5s (25p) for a second class ticket, while in 1875 a cheap excursion ticket from Huntingdon to 'Peterboro Agricultural Society's Show' cost 1s 6d (7p).

Left: *Peterborough's first railway line was served by the East Station, which was located on the south bank of the Nene, east of the Town Bridge. The development of the railways had an enormous effect on the growth of the city.*

The Modern City Emerges

Above: New machinery was introduced to the brick yards in the later Victorian period, and by 1900 over 1,500 men were employed there.

Above: John Thompson was a master builder, whose company specialised in cathedral restoration. He rebuilt the tower of Peterborough Cathedral between 1883 and 1890. A well-known local personality, Thompson was elected Mayor four times.

In the early 1880s a new process was developed at Fletton that allowed house bricks to be mass produced from the lower Oxford clay. With the excavation of the clay came the discovery of enormous fossilised bones of the sea creatures that 150 million years before had swum in the Jurassic sea covering the area.

Brick-making had been a local seasonal craft industry since the early 1800s, but now there was an increasing demand for bricks to build homes for Victorian Peterborough's growing population. With the new method, mass production could take place very cheaply, and the efficiency of the railways meant that the brick yards could supply even the London builders. The brick-making industry grew rapidly, with some small yards and some very large ones, but by the mid 1920s they were nearly all controlled by the London Brick Company.

The health and welfare of Peterborough's citizens was improved by local charities and an enlightened gentry.

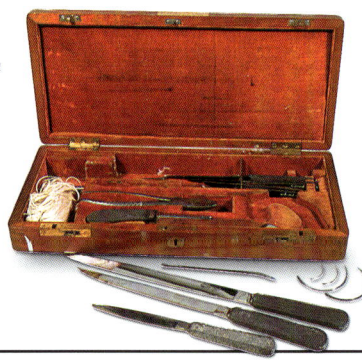

Right: A set of late Victorian surgical instruments, used at Peterborough Infirmary.

24

In 1816 a public dispensary opened, providing free medical treatment for those who could not afford to pay a doctor. Rural patients were accommodated at the newly built infirmary in Priestgate, the first modern city hospital. Dr T.J. Walker, the new infirmary's surgeon from 1862 to 1906, was the first Peterborian to be made a freeman of Peterborough in recognition of his contribution to the city.

Under the 1834 Poor Law Amendment Act, the very poor and the very sick were no longer given help to stay in their own homes, but had to be cared for in a workhouse by the local Poor Union. The Act segregated men, women and children, and the Peterborough Board of Guardians quickly realised that Wortley's workhouse, now almost a hundred years old, would be unsuitable. A new workhouse was built on Thorpe Road, and remained in use until the system was abolished in 1930.

The Improvement Commissioners had done what they could to develop the city, but in 1874 it became a municipal borough, able to elect a Council of six aldermen and eighteen councillors who would agree and finance major developments. The Council bought the 'Chamber over the Cross' from the Feoffees, and renamed it the Guildhall. Within five years, they constructed a new water and sewage system, reorganised the police service and began the long struggle to bring electric lighting to the city.

At around this time, a large number of new schools opened in the city, joining those already established in the early 1800s. Some of these were founded by Church groups to provide education for the families of ordinary working people, while others were privately run for children of the better-off.

Above: *A modern view of the brick works at Whittlesey – the last of an important local industry that bloomed throughout the last century.*

Left: *This building, originally constructed as a private house in 1816, served as the city and district infirmary between 1857 and 1928. Today it houses the collection of the Peterborough Museum & Art Gallery.*

A Century of Changes

By the early 20th century, Peterborough had become a centre of engineering excellence and a developing city with a rapidly growing population. Much of its prosperity arose from the substantial railway engineering works at New England, while farming also provided employment as large food-processing companies bought up locally grown produce. The historic quarries expanded as demand for stone, gravel and clay grew throughout the century. New industries began to move to Peterborough, building their factories on the green fields around the city. Baker Perkins and Peter Brotherhood, both manufacturers of industrial machinery, became major employers, and local manufacturing companies developed and grew.

The two World Wars brought many changes to the inhabitants of the Peterborough area. Those who fought and died in the Great War were commemorated by the building of a new hospital. Edith Cavell, who had been a pupil-teacher at Laurel Court School in the city, is also commemorated – she was executed by the Germans in 1915 for aiding the escape of resistance fighters from Belgium.

The flat, open countryside around Peterborough made an ideal location for airfields. RAF Wittering was established as a Home Defence Force airfield during the First World War. During the Second

Above: *In 1932 Frank Perkins and Charles Chapman set up a factory in Peterborough to design and build a high-speed diesel engine. By 1960, Perkins Engines had become the largest employer in the area, with over 7,000 staff. Today, they produce over 300,000 engines a year.*

 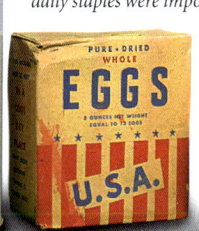

Below: *Food rationing was an unwelcome feature of the 'Home Front' during the Second World War. Some powdered versions of daily staples were imported.*